# Accessing ... RE:
## Buildings, Places and Artefacts A
### Christianity, Islam and Judaism

**Mainstream Teacher Book**

### Contents

| | |
|---|---|
| Introduction | 2 |
| Teachers' Notes | 3 |
| Christianity | 4 |
| Islam | 14 |
| Judaism | 24 |

**Eileen Osborne**

# Introduction

This book is based on a number of images. Those images, and the text used to link them, are meant to be used in a variety of ways. You could use them to give more depth and understanding to the topic of the lesson or they could be used to challenge students and give them the skills to become more effective, independent learners.

The written tasks and the briefing pages have been used specifically to increase the level of challenge, to encourage greater learning independence and to demand more abstract and precise use of language than 'middle ability' students might be able to cope with. The idea is that where more is demanded then more will be given – and the middle ability student can, in this respect, move onwards to reach higher levels of answering and thinking.

In this book, for the 'middle ability' students, some of the higher level skills have been used to make the tasks more demanding and encourage the students to look 'outside the box' for their answers. However, it must be remembered that students are looking at the buildings, places and artefacts of three of the world's main religions and in doing this they are expected to reflect on them and the influence on the religion they have had and continue to have. Religion is not just about buildings, places and artefacts – it is about the very fabric of what makes us human, what makes us 'tick', and the images and text throughout this series bear this in mind.

This, the seventh book in the series, has 'Buildings, Places and Artefacts' as its focus. Examining, as it does, the buildings, places and artefacts of Christianity, Islam and Judaism, it enables students to see 'behind' them in order to begin to understand the background and realise the contributions the buildings, places and artefacts have made to the faiths and beliefs of individuals and communities. In many ways the pages will allow students to evaluate the impact of the buildings, places and artefacts on the lives of the believers. Students are also encouraged to ask the 'Why' and 'How' questions in detail in such a way as to open up avenues of understanding for them.

In current educational debate 'challenge is the prerequisite of learning' and for the middle ability student this must enable them to move forward in their thinking while giving them opportunities to look beyond their horizons and become more confident learners and thinkers. I hope that this book will enable teacher and student alike to increase the level of challenge in RE lessons while at the same time learning more about the major faiths in the world today.

The images chosen to link with this have been carefully selected to reflect various schools of thought within the world faiths outlined. There is no intention to cause offence with any of them.

*Eileen Osborne 2005*

# Teachers' Notes

Using the support materials

The support materials are based on the images in the student's colour book. There are three levels of support materials and the tasks given for each level are meant to both support and extend students.

The three levels of materials, which can be distinguished by the use of the following symbols, are meant for:

   Gifted and Talented/More able students

   Middle and Average ability students

   Less able students

For all students the emphasis is on 'challenge' and students are required to think above and beyond the low order skills of knowledge and comprehension. Questions are asked which lead them to think 'outside the box', so leading to the middle order skill of application and then on to the higher order skills of analysis, synthesis and evaluation.

The activities have been varied but they all offer students the chance to look at the buildings, places and artefacts of the religions covered in a way that encourages independence of learning, abstract thinking and open-ended tasks.

The materials presume that students have little or no knowledge of the buildings, places and artefacts featured and so could best be used to start looking in depth at the topic. For weaker readers it is expected that the teacher will read the materials, with students following the text.

In cases where the text mentions the image only in passing, the teacher may wish to extend the learning in class by looking at the image in more detail in a subsequent lesson or setting a homework task for it.

On many pages students are asked to give their opinions about the image shown and, in some cases, to interpret the image through the eyes of the artist. This will enable all levels of students to speculate and hypothesise, thus adding to the 'culture of challenge' when using the materials.

This book is intended as a resource for teachers to photocopy as they wish. For some activities scissors, glue, A3/4 plain paper and coloured pens/pencils will be needed.

# Christianity

**Photo Book reference**: Page 4

## Briefing Sheet
## Why is the Church of the Nativity sacred to Christians?

**Q** *Why is the Church of the Nativity special to Christians?*

**A** *It marks the site of Jesus' birthplace.*

**Q** *Where is it?*

**A** *In the centre of Bethlehem, 8 kilometres from Jerusalem.*

**Q** *Where is it in Bethlehem?*

**A** *It is on Manger Square.*

**Q** *Why is it built like a fortress?*

**A** *Because it has been fought over for centuries.*

**Q** *How is the actual site of Jesus' birth marked?*

**A** *By a 14-point star on a marble stone.*

- The Roman Emperor, Constantine, declared Christianity as the religion of the Roman Empire in 325 CE.
- He ordered Bishop Makarios of Jerusalem to build a church over the site of the birthplace of Jesus.
- The church was completed by 333 CE but was burnt down in 529 CE.
- The Emperor Justinian ordered a new church to be built and the rebuilding was completed by 565 CE.

This is what a Spanish pilgrim, a priest named Jacinthus, wrote about the church in the 11th century:

*'A glorious building: it has no better. No palace in the world is equal in beauty.'*

*To get into the church you have to go through the Door of Humility. This doorway is very small so that visitors have to bend over when going through it. It is said to have been done to stop men on their horses from entering the church!*

*Accessing ... RE: Buildings, Places and Artefacts*

*Briefing and Activity Sheet*

# What important Christian sites are there in Jerusalem?

**Photo Book reference**: Pages 5–6

*Jerusalem was given its name by King David. The word means 'City of Peace'.*

Jerusalem is the most sacred city for Christians. The Bible records that Jesus was taken there as a baby and as a child of 12. He spent the final days of His life there and the Last Supper, Crucifixion and Resurrection all happened in the city. There are many Christian shrines/sites in Jerusalem:

- The Church of the Holy Sepulchre marking the site of the Resurrection
- Golgotha (Calvary), the site of the Crucifixion
- Mount of Olives where Jesus ascended into heaven
- The Garden of Gethsemane where Jesus was arrested
- The Via Dolorosa or 'Way of Sorrows' which follows Jesus' route through the city to Golgotha.

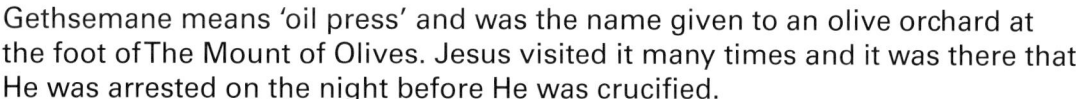

The Church of the Holy Sepulchre was built on the orders of the Roman Emperor, Constantine.
His mother, Queen Helena, had found the site and by 335 CE a massive church had been built which covered the sites of the Holy Sepulchre and Golgotha (Calvary). This church was destroyed in 614 CE.
When the Crusaders entered Jerusalem in 1099 CE one of their first tasks was to rebuild the church. It took 50 years for this – the church was finally completed in 1149 CE.

Gethsemane means 'oil press' and was the name given to an olive orchard at the foot of The Mount of Olives. Jesus visited it many times and it was there that He was arrested on the night before He was crucified.

**Examine the evidence**
Look at the images on pages 5 and 6.

1. Describe what you can see in the image of the Church of the Holy Sepulchre.

2. How can you tell that it is an important place?

3. Why do you think Jesus went to the Garden of Gethsemane so often?
   *Total time allowed 15 minutes.*

4. Imagine you were a Christian pilgrim visiting the two sites for the first time. Write down your feelings at being there and how the visit affected you.
   *Time allowed 5 minutes.*

5. Design a poster for either of the two sites you have looked at. The aim of the poster is to advertise the site for tourists. Make it colourful with reasons why the tourists should visit it.
   *Time allowed 30 minutes.*

**Accessing ... RE: Buildings, Places and Artefacts**

*Briefing and Activity Sheet*

# When did Christianity come to England? What were the early churches like?

**Photo Book reference**: Page 7

- Christianity first came to England in Roman times – probably brought by Roman traders or soldiers.
- From the late 5th century the Anglo-Saxons took control – they were not Christians.
- In 597 CE Pope Gregory decided that he wanted to convert the Anglo-Saxons to Christianity so he sent St Augustine and other monks to Britain to start the work.
- Augustine worked mainly in the south of England – he sent a monk named Paulinus to the north to bring Christianity to the rulers of Northumberland.
- Eventually the whole of Britain became Christian and many churches were built.

The church of St John's at Escomb is an important Anglo-Saxon church dating to between 600 and 800 CE. It is built of rubble and is little altered from when it was built.

**Examine the evidence**
Look at the image of the Anglo-Saxon church at Escomb on page 7.

1. Describe the church.

2. How can you tell this is a very old church?

3. Why do you think the church was built of stone at a time when buildings were usually built of wattle and daub?
   *Total time allowed 15 minutes.*

4. It is just after the church has been completed. You live near to it. You are not a Christian. What would you think of Christianity? What impression would the church have on you?
   *Time allowed 10 minutes.*

5. Design a stained-glass window for Escomb church on the theme of 'The Good Shepherd'.
   *Time allowed 25 minutes.*

*Accessing ... RE: Buildings, Places and Artefacts*

*Briefing and Activity Sheet*

# Why is Lindisfarne or Holy Island an important site for Christians?

**Photo Book reference**: Page 8

- Lindisfarne was given its name by the first Anglo-Saxons who lived there.
- The monks of Durham gave it another name – Holy Island – because of the monastery and monks who lived and worked there.
- The island is off the north-east coast of England and many Christian pilgrims visit it especially during the summer months.

### 'The Apostle of Northumbria'

Aidan was a monk on the island of Iona when, in 633 CE, King Oswald of Northumbria invited the monks of Iona to send a mission to Northumbria. Aidan arrived with other monks in 635 CE and the monastery on Lindisfarne was started. From there the monks went out on their mission, which was to convert the people of the area to the Christian faith. Many stories are told about him.

It is said that when pagans attacked Oswald's palace at Bamburgh they piled wood around the walls and set alight to the wood. Aidan prayed for help and the wind changed direction and blew the flames and smoke over the pagan army.

In another story, Oswald gave Aidan a horse to use but Aidan gave it away to a beggar, saying that he wanted to walk so that he would be on the same level as the people he met.

Aidan died in 651 CE at Bamburgh. The young St Cuthbert, a shepherd at the time, saw Aidan's soul rise to heaven as a shaft of light. Aidan was buried on Lindisfarne.

### Examine the evidence
Look at the image of St Aidan on page 8.

1. Describe Aidan as shown in the image.

2. What is he holding in his hands? What do you think they symbolise?

3. Why do you think he chose to start his monastery on Lindisfarne rather than on the mainland?
   *Total time allowed 15 minutes.*

4. Use the shape of Lindisfarne, shown here, as a background, and illustrate what St Cuthbert saw, i.e. Aidan's spirit going to heaven as a shaft of light. What does this tell you about Aidan?
   *Time allowed 30 minutes.*

*Accessing ... RE: Buildings, Places and Artefacts* — **7**

*Briefing and Activity Sheet*

# What are the common features of Christian churches?

**Photo Book reference**: Pages 9–10

Churches are often the oldest buildings in a local area. Some churches are very old, for example St Martin's in Canterbury was in use when St Augustine landed in 597 CE and some are very new, for example the Trinity Centre in North Ormesby, Middlesbrough. Whatever the age or design of the church, it serves one main purpose – to worship God.

### Facts and figures

- The Church of England or Anglican Church has around 16,000 church buildings and 43 cathedrals in 13,000 parishes covering the whole of England. That is just one branch of the Christian Church in England!
- Many churches were built in the shape of the cross. Many modern churches are built 'in the round'.
- No matter what the shape or size, they are all used by Christians for worship and for the life events we all take part in – child baptisms, weddings and funerals. They are often used as centres for the whole community.
- In a recent survey 86% of those asked said that they had been in a church in the previous 12 months for various reasons.

### Examine the evidence
Look at the image on page 9 showing the inside of Canterbury Cathedral.

1. Describe what you can see in the image. Make sure you mention the size and the height of the building.

2. How do you know this is an important building?
   *Total time allowed 10 minutes.*

Look at the two images on page 10.
3. Describe both churches.

4. What is the same about both churches and what is different?

5. Which church do you prefer and why?
   *Total time allowed 15 minutes.*

6. Design a church for the 21st century! Make a detailed drawing of it from the outside and then a bird's eye plan from the inside.
   *Time allowed 20 minutes.*

> **Remember** – not all churches will look the same!
> Some churches or places of worship are very plain, for example a Citadel for the Salvation Army, while others are full of statues and images, for example a Roman Catholic Church.

*Accessing ... RE: Buildings, Places and Artefacts*

## Activity Sheet
# What are the insides of churches like?

**Photo Book reference**: Pages 11–12

*The word church comes from a Greek word 'ekklesia'. This word means the people who believe rather than a building. However, the word has come to mean the building in which Christians gather.*

*The word cathedra means the 'seat of a bishop' so a cathedral is the place where a bishop has his throne.*

### Examine the evidence
Look at the two images on page 11.

1. Describe the inside of the Apostolic Church. Make sure you mention what is on the walls and what 'furniture' is there.
   *Time allowed 10 minutes.*

Now look at the other image on page 11. It shows the altar of the Cathedral of Santiago de Compostela in Spain.
2. Describe what you can see.
   *Time allowed 10 minutes.*

3. How are the insides of the two places of worship different? What does that tell you about the worshippers?
   *Time allowed 10 minutes.*

Now look at the two images on page 12.
4. Describe what you can see. What do the images tell you about the churches they are in?
   *Time allowed 10 minutes.*

5. People often donate a stained-glass window or candlesticks or an image to a church. Why do you think they do this?
   *Time allowed 10 minutes.*

6. Which of the images on pages 11 and 12 show your 'idea' of a church? Give reasons for your answer.
   *Time allowed 5 minutes.*

*'For centuries churches have been at the centre of the lives of the local communities they serve. Churches as such are a lasting part of our history and continue to be so.'*

**Accessing ... RE: Buildings, Places and Artefacts**

## Briefing and Activity Sheet
# What is special for Christians in Communion or Mass?

**Photo Book reference**: Page 13

*From the start of the Christian Church, believers have gathered together to 'break bread'.*

*Different words are used to describe this ceremony depending upon which branch of the Christian Church is involved.*

*Protestant groups refer to this as the Eucharist, Holy Communion, Sacrament, Breaking of Bread, and the Lord's Supper.*

*Roman Catholics and Anglo Catholics refer to it as the Mass.*

### Examine the evidence
Look at the images on page 13. They show Communion in the United Reformed Church and Mass in a Roman Catholic Church.

1. Describe each picture in detail.

2. What are the similarities and the differences in the pictures?
   *Total time allowed 15 minutes.*

3. Why do you think Christians have these ceremonies? Why and how are they important to the individual Christian?
   *Time allowed 10 minutes.*

4. The phrases shown below are used in various 'breaking of bread' services. Read them through and then write an explanation of what you think they mean.
   *Time allowed 5 minutes.*

> *'The peace of the Lord be with you.'*
>
> *'Go in peace to love and serve the Lord.'*

5. In some churches, where the small glasses are used for the 'wine', the congregation keep their glasses until everyone has been served and then they all drink together. What does this tell you about those churches?
   *Time allowed 10 minutes.*

*Briefing and Activity Sheet*

# Why are the cross and the rosary important artefacts to many Christians?

**Photo Book reference**: Page 14

The cross has become the main symbol of Christianity. It reminds Christians of the fact that Jesus died as a sacrifice for them and that He triumphed over death. The empty cross reminds Christians of this. Crucifixes – crosses with the figure of Jesus on them – are popular in Roman Catholic and Orthodox Churches.

- The Rosary is used mainly by Roman Catholics to remember and meditate on the main events in the life of Jesus.
- The beads are passed through the forefinger and thumb of both hands.
- The prayers which are said while doing this are the Lord's Prayer, the Hail Mary and the Gloria.

There are five sets of ten beads on the Rosary separated by larger beads. A cross or crucifix, on a set of four beads, is attached to the end.

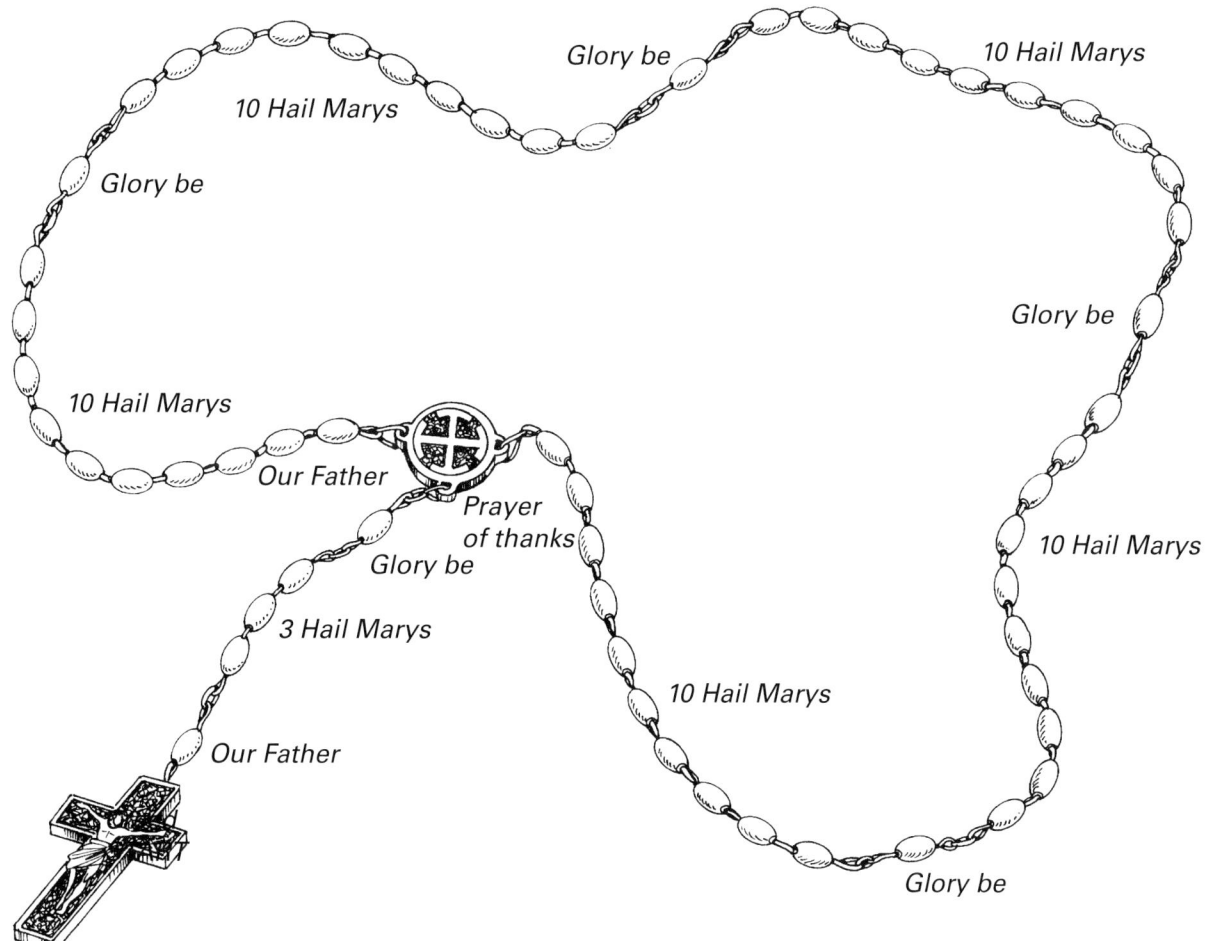

### Examine the evidence

1. The Rosary is used to help concentrate the mind. Do you think it will be difficult for Christians to pray or meditate? Give reasons for your answer.
   *Time allowed 10 minutes.*

2. Many people who are not Christians wear a cross or crucifix. Should they do this? Give reasons for your answer.
   *Time allowed 10 minutes.*

***Accessing ... RE: Buildings, Places and Artefacts***

## Briefing and Activity Sheet

# How is 'modern art' used in Christian places of worship?

**Photo Book reference**: Pages 15–16

> Coventry Cathedral was destroyed in 1940 by bombs dropped by the Luftwaffe.
> The next morning it was decided that the Cathedral had to be rebuilt.
> The foundation stone for the new Cathedral was laid in 1956.
> It was decided that it should be filled with works of art by leading artists.
> John Piper designed the Baptistry window and Epstein designed the images of St Michael and the Devil which are at the front of the Cathedral on the main steps.
> The rebuilt Cathedral was consecrated on 25 May 1962.

**Examine the evidence**
Look at page 15.

1. Describe what you think the picture shows. Note the chains around the body of the Devil and the way St Michael is standing over the Devil.

2. Do you think this is a good statue to have at the entrance to the Cathedral? Give reasons for your answer.
   *Total time allowed 10 minutes.*

Now look at page 16. If you look very closely you can see, just above the word Cathedral, the figure of a man. This gives you some idea of the size of this stained-glass window.

3. What does the window 'say' to you? Make sure you give your reasons.
   *Time allowed 10 minutes.*

4. Of the two works of art on pages 15 and 16 which one do you like best and why?
   *Time allowed 10 minutes.*

5. The ruins of the old Cathedral stand beside the rebuilt Cathedral. Why do you think this was done?
   *Time allowed 15 minutes.*

> Two of the roof timbers from the old Cathedral had fallen together in the shape of a cross. They were set up in the ruins of the burnt out Cathedral. Later they were placed on an altar made from the rubble of the destroyed Cathedral and the words 'Father Forgive' were written.

6. What do those words mean? How are they linked to the cross made from the roof timbers?
   *Time allowed 10 minutes.*

*Accessing ... RE: Buildings, Places and Artefacts*

*Briefing and Activity Sheet*

# Why do Christians go on pilgrimage? What are the pilgrimage sites like?

**Photo Book reference**: Pages 17–18

### Lourdes

Many thousands of people visit Lourdes in France every year. It has been a centre for Christian pilgrimage for almost 150 years. A young girl named Bernadette Soubirous had a total of 18 apparitions of the Virgin Mary in a grotto at Lourdes. These happened between February and July in 1858. Since then many people have said that they have been healed or cured of various illnesses and diseases while at Lourdes.

**Examine the evidence**
Look at the image on page 17.

1. Describe what you can see.

2. What impression of Lourdes do you get from the image?

3. 'I wasn't cured but my faith grew 100-fold from going to Lourdes.'
   What do you think this 18-year-old girl meant by this statement?
   *Total time allowed 20 minutes.*

### Walsingham

Walsingham in Norfolk is also a centre for Christian pilgrimage. Richeldis de Faverches had a vision there in 1061. In the vision she was taken by Mary, the mother of Jesus, and was shown the house in Nazareth where the angel Gabriel had announced the news of Mary's pregnancy. Mary asked Richeldis to build an exact replica of that house in Walsingham. The vision was repeated three times. According to the story, the materials for the house were collected together and one night, while Richeldis was in prayer, the Holy House was reconstructed in Walsingham.

Walsingham became known as 'England's Nazareth'.

Every year thousands of Christian pilgrims travel to Walsingham, some looking for miracle cures while others go to renew and refresh their faith.

**Examine the evidence**
The image shows the statue of the Madonna and Child at Walsingham.

4. Describe the statue on page 18. Why do you think both Mary and the infant Jesus wear crowns? What book do you think the infant Jesus is holding? Mary holds a lily. What do you think it symbolises?
   *Time allowed 15 minutes.*

5. What kind of people do you think go on pilgrimage? Why do they go?

6. 'Miracles happen after visiting Walsingham. People are cured of illnesses, the unhappy are made happy, and those whose faith is lost find it again.'
   Do you think miracles can happen? Give reasons for your answer.
   *Total time allowed 15 minutes.*

**Accessing ... RE: Buildings, Places and Artefacts**

# Islam

**Photo Book reference**: Page 19

## Briefing and Activity Sheet
## Why is Makkah a holy city to Muslims?

**Examine the evidence**
Look at the image on page 19. It shows a sign post to Makkah, the most holy city of the Islamic faith.

1. What does the sign post tell you about Makkah?

2. Makkah is in Saudi Arabia. What does the background tell you about the land of Saudi Arabia?

3. The lettering on the sign is in both Arabic and English. Why do you think this is?
   *Total time allowed 15 minutes.*

### Facts and figures about Makkah

- The full name of Makkah is Makkah al-Mukkaramah.
- It has 1.4 million inhabitants (2003).
- It is 80km from the Red Sea coast.
- It is built around a natural well.
- Muslims believe it was the first place created on Earth by Allah.
- It is the place where Ibrahim and his son Isma'il built the Ka'ba.
- The Ka'ba is a rectangular building made of bricks and covered in a gold-embroidered black fabric.

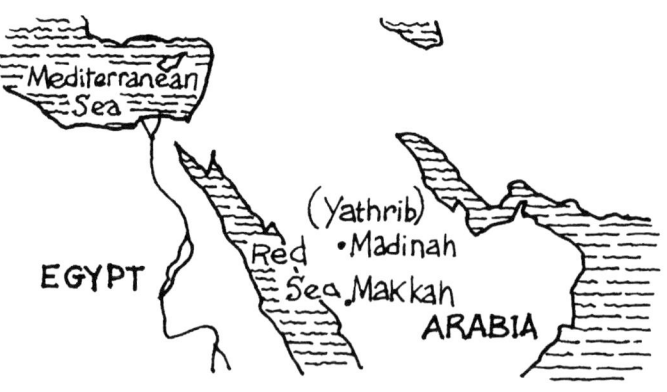

- A pilgrimage to Makkah is required by all Muslims who can afford to go.
- Every year about three million Muslims gather at Makkah for the Hajj or major pilgrimage.
- Every Muslim prays five times a day in the direction of Makkah.
- The prophet Muhammad was born in Makkah in 571 CE.

- Makkah is the focal point for all Muslims wherever they live.
- Muslims also travel to Makkah for the Umra or lesser pilgrimage.

**14** Accessing ... RE: Buildings, Places and Artefacts

**Briefing and Activity Sheet**

# What do Muslims do while on pilgrimage to Makkah?

**Photo Book reference:** Pages 20–21

Ali is a 15-year-old Muslim boy. He went to Makkah for the first time last year. Read what he says about his pilgrimage:

> I was very excited by the time we got to Makkah. The next day we circled the Ka'ba seven times and I touched and then kissed the Black Stone! The black cloth or Kiswah which covers the Ka'ba was raised up for the pilgrimage.
>
> We ran between the two hills, As Safa and Al Marwa. We visited the Zamzam Well and I dipped the edge of my ihram in the water and so did my father, brother and grandfather. We collected some of the water in a container to take home with us.
>
> The most difficult time for me during the pilgrimage was the 'Stand before Allah' at 'Arafat because it was very hot and we were there for quite a long time.
>
> The next day we were at Mina and we 'Stoned the Devil'. This means I threw seven small stones at a pillar which is named 'The Great Devil'. There was the sacrifice of an animal at Mina and then finally I had my head shaved. In some ways I was very tired after Hajj but in other ways I was wide awake – my faith had grown stronger and I had been with Muslims from all over the world and we were all united as brothers.

**Q** *Imagine you are a non-Muslim friend of Ali's. What questions would you want to ask him about his pilgrimage when he returned to England?*
*Time allowed 10 minutes.*

**Examine the evidence**
The image on page 20 shows the encircling of the Ka'ba in Makkah.

1. Describe what you can see.

2. How do you think the individual Muslim will feel at seeing all the millions of other pilgrims there?
   *Total time allowed 15 minutes.*

3. What kind of a city is Makkah? Make sure you give your reasons.

4. Only Muslims are allowed into Makkah. Why do you think this is?

5. What do you think would happen if a non-Muslim tried to get into this most holy of Muslim cities?
   *Total time allowed 15 minutes.*

The image on page 21 shows the Black Stone in its silver surround. This is a very ancient stone – possibly a meteorite. If any pilgrims cannot get near enough to touch or kiss it they raise their hand to it as they go round. Pilgrims go round in an anti-clockwise direction seven times.

6. Look at the image. Describe what you can see.

7. There are many rituals associated with the Hajj. How important do you think these are to Muslims? Give reasons for your answers.
   *Total time allowed 15 minutes.*

**Accessing ... RE: Buildings, Places and Artefacts**

## Briefing and Activity Sheet

# Why is Madinah an important city for Muslims?

**Photo Book reference**: Page 22

The image on page 22 shows the centre of Madinah with The Prophet's Mosque in the centre. The first two Caliphs, Abu Bakr and 'Umar, were buried next to Muhammad in the place that had originally been the Prophet's home. Today it is covered by the green dome of the mosque – in the centre of the picture.

**Examine the evidence**
Look at the image closely.

1. Describe the city from what you can see in the picture.

2. There are two minarets in the picture – both have loudspeakers fitted to them. What do you think is the purpose of the loudspeakers?
   *Total time allowed 10 minutes.*

---

### More about Madinah

- Its full name is Al-Madinah Al-Munawarah.
- It is the city which supported Muhammad when he left Makkah.
- It is the second most holy place for Muslims.
- Many Muslims visit Madinah each year.
- The Prophet's Mosque was built just after Muhammad had migrated to the city in 622 CE.
- The city was originally called 'Yathrib'.
- The Prophet's Mosque today is 100 times the size it was when Muhammad and his companions first built it.
- It can hold half a million worshippers.
- There is even an underground car park designed to hold 5,000 cars.

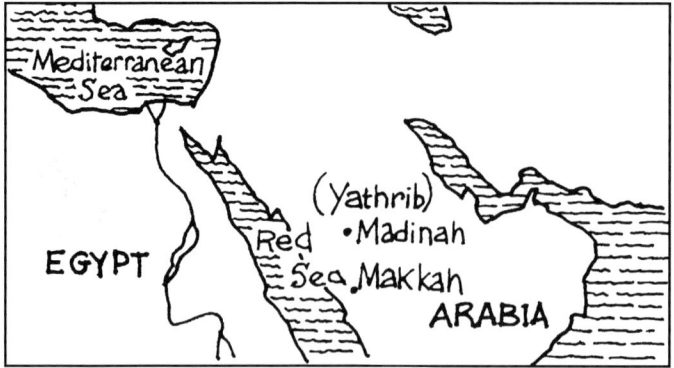

### *How was the site of the first mosque chosen?*

Muhammad let his camel loose and allowed it to wander. Where it finally stopped was the chosen site of the mosque. All the people of the city, plus those who had migrated from Makkah with Muhammad, helped in the building of that first mosque.

**Accessing ... RE: Buildings, Places and Artefacts**

*Briefing and Activity Sheet*

# Why is Jerusalem a holy city for Muslims?

**Photo Book reference**: Page 23

- In 619 CE Muhammad's wife Khadijah, and his uncle, Abu Talib, both died.
- It was a sad time for Muhammad and Muslims believe that at that very low time in his life, Allah took Muhammad up to heaven.
- The story is that one night Muhammad travelled from Makkah to Jerusalem on the winged horse, Buraq, to a spot called the 'Further Mosque'.
- From a rock in Jerusalem, Muhammad then went up to heaven.
- In heaven he spoke to the prophets and even approached the throne of Allah.
- He brought back from the journey the command to pray five times a day.
- This event is called 'The Night Journey' and the spot in Jerusalem from where Muhammad went up to heaven now has the Dome of the Rock built over it.

Caliph 'Umar built a mosque on the spot in 638 CE. The Mosque in the image was built in 687 CE and covers the rock from which Muhammad went to heaven. The Dome of the Rock is a shrine rather than a mosque. Later a mosque was built near to the Dome of the Rock site and was named 'The Further Mosque' or Al-Aksa Mosque. Muslims believe that prayers in that mosque are equal to 500 prayers in any other ordinary mosque.

For Muslims, Jerusalem is the third most holy site in Islam after Makkah and Madinah. Muslim tradition states that the area of Jerusalem and Makkah will be connected together at the end of time – the Day of Judgement.

### Examine the evidence
Look at the image on page 23.

1. How can you tell this is an important Muslim shrine?
   *Time allowed 10 minutes.*

2. Look closely at the decoration on the walls of the building. Decoration is either calligraphy or patterns. Copy one of those patterns onto A3-sized paper and colour it. Why do Muslims not draw people?
   *Time allowed 20 minutes.*

*Briefing and Activity Sheet*

# What are the common features seen in every mosque?

**Photo Book reference**: Pages 24–31

**Examine the evidence**
Look at the mosques shown on pages 24, 25 and 27.

1. How are they the same?

2. How are they different?

3. What does this tell you about Islam and Muslims? Here's a clue – take note of the places where these mosques are!
   *Total time allowed 20 minutes.*

Now look at the mosque on page 26.

4. Describe what you can see.

5. How is this mosque different to the three others? What does this tell you about Baluchistan?
   *Total time allowed 10 minutes.*

---

No matter what the size of the mosque there will be features inside which every mosque has. These are:

- No seats in the prayer hall. The prayer hall is for men only – see the image on page 29.
- The women's worship area is away from the men's and is usually much smaller.
- Spaces to put shoes, as outdoor shoes are removed before going into the prayer hall.
- Facilities for washing, as Muslims must wash before entering the prayer hall – see the image on page 30.
- A mihrab, an alcove in the wall which tells Muslims the direction of Makkah. They must face Makkah when they pray – see the image on page 31.
- A mimbar where the imam will preach from – see the image on page 31.
- The mosques may be decorated with patterns and calligraphy. There will be no pictures, images or statues. Some mosques are plain inside with no decoration at all.
- Many mosques have at least one minaret (tower) and it is from there that the call to prayer is given. A muezzin used to climb the tower to give the call to prayer. Nowadays loudspeakers are used – and often the call to prayer is pre-recorded – see the images on page 28.
- The mosque will also have other rooms apart from those mentioned above.
- Rooms will be used for teaching and learning and for community meetings.
- There will also be a room where the dead are brought to be prepared for burial.

*Accessing ... RE: Buildings, Places and Artefacts*

## Briefing and Activity Sheet

# What else do I need to know about a mosque?

**Photo Book reference**: Pages 24–31

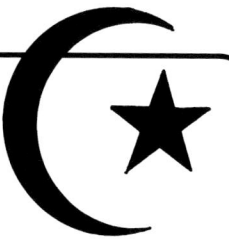

A mosque is a house of prayer. The Arabic name is 'masjid' which means 'place of prostration'. There are no hard and fast rules for what a mosque should be like – the only 'rules' are that there should be a clear indication of the direction of Makkah (this direction is called qibla). In most mosques this means a mihrab, an alcove in the wall. There must be a roofed area in front of the mihrab and there must be no doors on the wall where the mihrab is. Another feature in all mosques is the mimbar or pulpit from where the Friday prayer and sermon are held.

In the early years of Islam, just after the death of Muhammad, the Muslim conquerors always built a mosque before anything else. The military camp was then built around the mosque.

The minaret was developed so that the muezzin could make the call to prayer heard. If the call was made from ground level it did not carry very well.

Inside the mosque the worshippers kneel in rows parallel to the qibla wall. The mimbar is to the side of the mihrab.

### Examine the evidence
Look at the images on page 28.

1. What are the differences in the minarets shown?

2. What do these differences tell you about the countries where they are used?
   *Total time allowed 10 minutes.*

Look at page 29.
3. Describe what you can see. What kind of atmosphere do you 'feel' from the image?
   *Time allowed 10 minutes.*

Page 30 shows the times of prayer on a sign outside a mosque and Muslims washing before going into the mosque.
4. What do you think Muslims wash before going into the Mosque?

5. Why do you think they are told when to pray? What are they trying to do by this?
   *Total time allowed 10 minutes.*

Page 31 shows a mihrab and a mimbar.
6. Describe what you can see.

7. Notice how the areas are decorated in both images. Notice how the mimbar and mihrab are decorated. How would you describe those decorations?
   *Total time allowed 15 minutes.*

8. Using what you have learnt about a mosque, write a 'Guide to a mosque' for Year 6 pupils. Make it colourful and full of facts. You could also include a wordsearch or a quiz about the mosque.
   *This may have to be done as homework.*

**Accessing ... RE: Buildings, Places and Artefacts**

### Briefing and Activity Sheet

# What uses does a mosque have?

**Photo Book reference**: Pages 24–31

A mosque plays a very important role in the lives of Muslims. The main function is for prayer, but there are other roles it may play. Read what Ali and his brother Hassan say about their mosque.

> Our mosque has a madrash or Islamic school. There are Arabic classes for children and adults. We are taught how to study the Qur'an. I go twice a week for this. We also go for various activities, a bit like a youth club. My mother attends a class about the family. The mosque is much more than a place for prayer – it is there to help the whole Muslim community. There are counsellors to help if you have a problem, you can go for advice about health matters. There is even a kindergarten for the really young children.
>
> — *Ali*:

> Our mosque is really more like a home to us. I use the library a lot and I also buy books from the bookshop. Sometimes we have non-Muslims in as visitors to find out more about what it means to be a Muslim. A few weeks ago there were some trainee teachers who came along and spent time with us – they asked a lot of questions about what it means to be a Muslim. Sometimes we have classes from local schools that come in to learn more about Islam.
>
> — *Hassan*:

### Examine the evidence

1. Use what Hassan and Ali have said about their mosque to create a chart which shows the uses a mosque may have. Put the ages of the people who will use each facility you mention. Add any other uses you might know of.
   *Time allowed 15 minutes.*

2. Why is it important for Muslim children to learn Arabic?

3. Is it important for non-Muslims to visit the mosque? Give reasons for your answer.
   *Total time allowed 10 minutes.*

4. Imagine you are a teacher taking a group of Year 7 pupils to a mosque. What 'rules and regulations' would you give to your pupils before the visit. For each of your rules and regulations say why you would give them.
   *Time allowed 15 minutes.*

*Briefing and Activity Sheet*

# What happens at prayer time?

**Photo Book reference**: Pages 30 and 32–33

**Q** *How many times a day should a Muslim pray?*

**A** *The Five Pillars of Islam state that all Muslims should pray five times a day.*

**Q** *What are the ritual prayers called in Arabic?*

**A** *Salah.*

**Q** *What are the five times of prayer?*

**A** *Between dawn and sunrise, after midday, in the late afternoon, just after sunset, at night.*

**Q** *What are these prayer times in Arabic?*

**A** *Fajr, Zuhr, Asr, Maghrib, Isha.*

**Q** *Why are there six times shown on the picture on page 30?*

**A** *The sixth time is that of the Friday prayer – the Jum'ah prayer which is said instead of the Zuhr prayer.*

**Q** *Who should go to the mosque on a Friday?*

**A** *All Muslim men should attend on a Friday.*

**Q** *What about Muslim women?*

**A** *Women do not have to attend the mosque.*

> All Muslims must perform wudu before they pray (they must wash in a certain way and be correctly clothed for prayer). Page 22 gives more information about wudu.

**Examine the evidence**
Look at page 32. It shows a prayer compass and a prayer mat.

1. What do you think the compass is used for?

Every prayer mat must have an arch design on it so that it can be laid in the correct direction for prayer, that is facing the Ka'ba in Makkah. Prayer mats are usually decorated in Islamic patterns.

2. Describe the prayer mat. Why do you think a Muslim uses a prayer mat? *Total time allowed 10 minutes.*

**Accessing ... RE: Buildings, Places and Artefacts**

*Briefing Sheet*

# What must a Muslim do before and during prayer?

**Photo Book reference**: Pages 31–33

### Getting ready for prayer – wudu

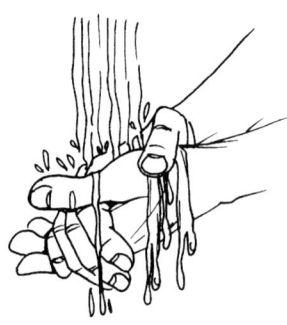

1. Wash the hands.

2. Rinse out the mouth three times.

3. Take water up into the nose and blow it out three times.

4. Wash all the face three times using both hands.

5. Wash the right arm then the left from wrist to elbow three times.

6. Rub the back of the head with wet hands, then the neck then the ears inside and out.

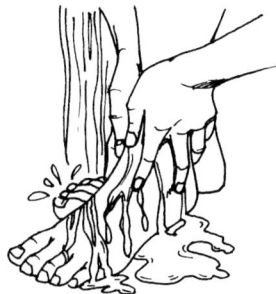

7. Wash the right foot to the ankle and then the left to the ankle.

### Clothing for prayer

- Shoes must be removed.
- Men must be covered at least to their knees.
- Women must cover themselves and wear a scarf on their heads.
- Only the face and hands of a woman should be uncovered.
- Most men will wear a prayer cap (see page 33) although it is not compulsory.

**Remember**:
A Muslim does not have to repeat wudu for each set of prayers unless s/he has been to the toilet or been to sleep between times. If there is no water to hand, the Muslim can use sand or even dust for wudu.

## Briefing and Activity Sheet
# What are prayer beads and prayer caps?

**Photo Book reference**: Page 33

### Subhah are Muslim prayer beads.

Sometimes they are also called tasbih but this is more the praying with the beads rather than the beads themselves. The word tasbih means 'To praise God' or 'To pray to God'.

- There are 99 beads on the thread.
- The 99 beads are divided into three sets of 33 – each set is divided by other slightly different beads.
- Muslims use the beads to recite the Ninety-Nine Beautiful Names of Allah.
- The prayer beads are finished off with a tassel.
- The beads are passed between the forefinger and the thumb.
- Some Muslims use the beads to repeat phrases about Allah.
- With the first 33 beads passing through their finger and thumb they repeat 'Subhan Allah', 'Glory be to Allah', 33 times.
- With the next 33 beads they repeat 'Alhamdu lillah', 'All praise be to Allah', 33 times.
- With the final set of 33 beads they repeat 'Allahu Akbar' 'God is great' 33 times.

### Examine the evidence
Look at the prayer beads shown on page 33.

1. What can you learn about the beads from this picture?

2. Why are prayer beads used by Muslims?

3. What do you think the purpose is of repeating the same three phrases?
   *Total time allowed 15 minutes.*

When Muslims go on Hajj to Makkah they can buy special prayer beads which are black and white and bring them back as gifts.
Subhah made from the clay of Makkah or Madinah are prized possessions.

A kufi is a prayer cap worn by Muslim males. It is also called a keffiyeh. Muslim men are not required to cover their hair but doing so is recommended. It was the practice of Muhammad and his Companions to cover their heads. It is considered 'mustahab' or 'praiseworthy' to cover the head during prayer.
A kufi can be in various styles and colours. Some are embroidered while others are plain woven cotton.

Look at the prayer cap shown on page 33.

4. Describe the cap.

5. Why do you think it is considered 'praiseworthy' to cover the head during prayer?
   *Total time allowed 15 minutes.*

# Judaism

**Photo Book reference**: Pages 34–36

## Briefing and Activity Sheet

## What is a synagogue?

- A Jewish place of worship is called a synagogue.
- Some Jews also call it shul (school) or bet haknesset (place of assembly) or temple.
- The synagogue is not just for worship. Many other activities take place there.
- It is more like a centre for the Jewish community.
- It is the place where Jews meet to worship God and study God's Law.

**Examine the evidence**

1. Pages 34–36 show different synagogues. Look at them all and then compare and contrast them.
   *Time allowed 20 minutes.*

2. The synagogue at the bottom of page 36 is very different to the other three. It is also the only one to have the Star of David in evidence. Why is the Star of David special to Jews? What other Jewish symbols might you see on a synagogue?
   *Time allowed 5 minutes.*

The synagogues shown are from different places in the world. From the outside they look different but inside they will follow the same basic plan.

In the 6th century BCE, many Jews were taken into captivity in Babylon. Having no temple for their worship they started to meet in their homes. This led to the building of special places for worship, i.e. synagogues. When the Jews returned from Babylon they built synagogues and these became the centres for worship in whatever town or village they were built in.

3. Why do you think the Jews in captivity needed special places for worship?
4. What were they trying to do by meeting together while they were in exile?
   *Total time allowed 10 minutes.*

### Synagogue facts

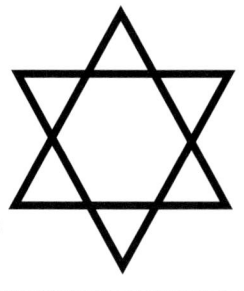

- The oldest synagogue in Europe is in Prague and dates from the 11th century.
- On Kristallnacht (Night of Broken Glass) 9 November 1938, the Nazis destroyed almost all the synagogues in Germany – 1574 in total.
- The oldest synagogue in the world has been found at Masada in Israel.
- The largest synagogue in the world is the Temple Emanu-El in New York. It has a floor area of 3,523 sq metres.

*Accessing ... RE: Buildings, Places and Artefacts*

*Briefing and Activity Sheet*

# What does the interior of a synagogue look like?

**Photo Book reference**: Pages 37–38

There are differences in the layout of a synagogue depending on whether it is Orthodox or Progressive Jews who use it.

In a Progressive synagogue the men and women will sit together while in an Orthodox synagogue the women will sit apart from the men, often in a women's gallery.

The seating in any synagogue is arranged so that everyone there can see the bimah. On the bimah there is a reading desk and it is on that desk the Torah Scrolls are placed when they are to be read to the congregation during worship.

Pictures or images are forbidden by Jewish Law but the inside of the synagogue may have stained glass windows and perhaps quotations written in Hebrew on the walls.

**Examine the evidence**
Look at the interior views of synagogues shown on pages 37 and 38.
The top image on page 37 is of a modern synagogue. The bottom image is of a much older synagogue.

1. Compare and contrast the two interiors.
   *Time allowed 15 minutes.*

Page 38 shows another two interiors.
2. Compare and contrast these two interiors.
   *Time allowed 15 minutes.*

3. There are many Jewish symbols to be found in the four images. Look carefully at them and write down the symbols you can see.

4. Why is it important to show these symbols in a synagogue?
   *Total time allowed 10 minutes.*

5. Look carefully at the top image on page 38. On the right-hand side there is a blue cloth with writing on it. Look carefully and read what it says. What does this tell you about the synagogue?

6. What are the common features in all four synagogues shown?
   *Total time allowed 10 minutes.*

Look again at the images. The main feature in a synagogue is the Ark, which is a decorated cabinet or cupboard that contains the Torah Scrolls. The Ark can be seen on all four images. Above the Ark are written the first words of the Ten Commandments.

7. Find out what those first words are and then say why you think they are written above the Ark.
   *Time allowed 10 minutes.*

*Accessing ... RE: Buildings, Places and Artefacts*

*Briefing Sheet*

# What are the main features inside a synagogue?

**Photo Book reference**: Pages 37–38

If you look closely at pages 37 and 38 you will see that the interior of a synagogue is similar in each picture.

These are the main features inside any synagogue:

- Ark: A decorated cabinet or cupboard which is placed in the centre of the main wall in the synagogue. It contains the Torah Scrolls. Above the Ark there are usually two tablets with the Ten Commandments written on them.
- In the centre of the synagogue is the bimah which is a raised platform with rails. The Torah is read from here.
- Above the Ark there is the ner tamid, the continual light. This is never allowed to go out.
- In front of the Ark is a pulpit which is used by the rabbi or invited speaker to speak to the congregation.
- In Orthodox synagogues, men sit in the main part and women and children sit in another part – usually an upstairs gallery.
- In Progressive synagogues, men and women sit together.

Other things you may see in a synagogue are:

- Star of David.
- Lions of Judah.

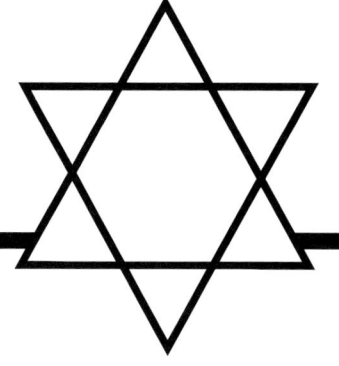

Whatever the synagogue looks like it is in continual use. It is a community centre, a school, a hall for large gatherings. There are often other rooms, for instance for parents and babies to use.

Some synagogues are very plain inside, for example the bottom picture on page 37; others have stained-glass windows and other decorations, for example the top picture on page 37.

Use pages 37 and 38 to look at the interior of a synagogue.

A synagogue is always built facing Jerusalem, the holy city of the Jews.

*Accessing ... RE: Buildings, Places and Artefacts*

*Briefing Sheet*

# Why is Israel a sacred land for the Jews?

**Photo Book reference**: Pages 39–42

Jews believe that the land of Israel is the 'Promised Land', promised to them by God. It is the 'Holy Land' and the city of Jerusalem is the 'Holy City'.

Jerusalem to the Jews is the centre of the world and they look to a time in the future when Jerusalem will be the city to which all nations will go, a place of justice. At that time the Temple in Jerusalem will be rebuilt and the Messiah, the 'Anointed One' will rule from Jerusalem in mercy and peace.

> *'I will give this land to your descendants.'*
> Genesis 12:7

- The Temple in Jerusalem was the focal point of Jewish worship.
- King Solomon built the first Temple – completed about 959 BCE – which was destroyed by the Babylonians in 586 BCE.
- Later another smaller Temple was built on the site when the people returned from exile.
- It was completed by 515 BCE.
- King Herod the Great started to build another Temple in 20 BCE and the site was not fully completed until 63 CE.
- The site measured about 400 metres by 300 metres.

### The building of Herod's Temple

There were 10,000 workers and 100 priests involved in the building of Herod's Temple. The main gate was the Golden Gate which had doors so huge that twenty men were needed to open them. The Temple itself was quite small but beautiful.

In 70 CE it was destroyed by the Romans after a Jewish rebellion. When the Temple existed Jews used it to offer sacrifice to God and it was also at the heart of many of their festivals.

Today all that remains of the Temple is part of its foundations. These foundations are called the 'Western Wall' or the 'Wailing Wall' because many who visit it are grief stricken to see that this is all that remains of their great Temple.

After the destruction of the Temple in 70 CE, the Jews were not allowed to visit the area where it had been. The whole area came under Muslim control and Jews were only allowed to visit it once a year on the anniversary of its destruction.

In 1967, during the Arab-Israeli War, the Israeli army captured the area of Jerusalem where the Temple had been, and from that time, Jews were able to visit the Wall as and when they wished. Today the site of the Temple is occupied by the Dome of the Rock and the Al Aqsa Mosque.

## Briefing and Activity Sheet

# What do I know about the Jewish holy sites in Israel?

**Photo Book reference**: Pages 39–42

### Examine the evidence
Page 39 shows a reconstruction of the Temple of Jerusalem built by King Herod.

1. Describe what you can see.

2. Why do you think Herod, who was only part Jewish, chose to build the Temple?

3. Why did the Romans destroy the Temple? Why not destroy a school or a market place?
   *Total time allowed 15 minutes.*

Look at page 40. It shows a satellite view of the land of Israel.
4. The Jews believe that God gave them this land. What therefore would be the Jewish attitude to the land of Israel?

5. Promised Land, Holy Land, Land of Milk and Honey are names given to Israel at various times. What does each of these names mean?
   *Total time allowed 15 minutes.*

Pages 41 and 42 show the Western or Wailing Wall. Look closely at them.
6. Describe what you can see on page 41.

7. In the centre of the image stands the Muslim Dome of the Rock with its golden dome. To the left there is a minaret. How do you think Jews and Muslims feel about sharing the sacred area and Jerusalem itself?

8. On page 42 you can see Jewish males at the Wailing Wall. Why is it such an important place for Jews? How do you think Jews feel about the fact that it is the only part of the Temple area left standing?
   *Total time allowed 15 minutes.*

Masada is considered to be a very special site for Jews. It is a great symbol for Jewish people. Israeli soldiers take an oath there 'Masada shall not fall again'. After Jerusalem and Yad Vashem, it is a very popular place to visit. After the Romans destroyed the Temple in 70 CE, 960 Jews held out for three years at Masada which is near the Dead Sea. The Roman army laid siege to Masada but as Masada is located at the top of a huge rock, anyone climbing it was seen by the Jewish defenders. However the Roman army eventually managed to breach the walls by building a huge ramp. The Jews at Masada chose death rather than being taken alive for slaves – the men first killed their wives and children then they killed themselves rather than give in to the Roman army. It is now, for Jews, a symbol of survival.

9. Why do you think Israeli soldiers take their oath on Masada?
   *Time allowed 10 minutes.*

*Accessing ... RE: Buildings, Places and Artefacts*

**Briefing and Activity Sheet**

# What is Yad Vashem?

**Photo Book reference**: Pages 43–44

Between 1933 and 1945 the Nazis murdered 6 million Jews. Many of those who died were gassed in concentration camps.

Yad Vashem was created to commemorate those 6 million Jews. Its task is to remind us all of what was done to the 6 million in the hope that it will never happen again. It is on the western outskirts of Jerusalem on the Hill of Remembrance. It is Israel's second most visited site after the Western Wall.

The Hall of Remembrance at Yad Vashem is a built of concrete with a low roof almost like a tent. It is empty apart from a flame which never goes out. Engraved on the floor are the names of the 21 Nazi extermination camps, concentration camps and killing sites in central and Eastern Europe. In front of the memorial flame there is a crypt which contains the ashes of many of those who were murdered.

Around 1.5 million children were murdered during the Holocaust. They are remembered in the Children's Memorial, an underground cavern in which one memorial candle is burnt. Cleverly placed mirrors create the illusion of an endless galaxy of flickering lights. A voice reads out the names of the children who were murdered. In that place there is no sound to be heard other than that voice.

On Holocaust Memorial Day many Jews visit Yad Vashem and light candles and say prayers.

**Examine the evidence**
Look at page 43. It shows the Hall of Remembrance.

1. Why do you think it has been kept so bare?

2. What do you think the eternal flame symbolises?

3. Write a description of the Hall from what you can see in the image and from what has been written about it above.
   *Total time allowed 20 minutes.*

Now look at page 44. This shows a memorial sculpture at Yad Vashem. Look closely at it.
4. Describe what you can see. Note the hands in the sculpture.

5. What do you think the sculpture is 'saying'? What questions would you want to ask the person who made it if you met?

6. Do you think it is a suitable sculpture for Yad Vashem? Make sure you give your reasons.
   *Total time allowed 20 minutes.*

**Accessing ... RE: Buildings, Places and Artefacts**

## Briefing and Activity Sheet

# What objects are associated with prayer in Judaism?

**Photo Book reference**: Pages 45–47

### The tallit or prayer shawl

- Made out of natural materials.
- It is a four-cornered square.
- It symbolises the fact that God is all around.
- It is white or cream with black or blue stripes at each end.
- There are fringes known as tzizit attached to each of the four corners.
- Before wearing it a blessing is repeated:

*'Blessed are you, the Lord our God, ruler of the universe, who has made us holy with His commandments and commanded us to wrap ourselves in fringes.'*

### Examine the evidence

Page 45 shows a group of Jewish girls and a Jewish boy wearing the tallit.

1. The tallit will eventually be used as a burial cloth for its owner. What does this tell you about it?

2. Why do you think a tallit is usually given as a Bar Mitzvah gift?

3. Compare and contrast the girls in the top image with the boy in the bottom image.
   *Total time allowed 20 minutes.*

### Skull cap or yamulkah

Some Jewish men wear one all the time to remind them that God is above them. Others wear them only for prayer because Jews are commanded to cover their heads as a symbol of respect to God. All men cover their heads when entering a synagogue.

Skull caps can be plain or decorated and are made out of many different materials, for example velvet, cotton or satin. Some Jewish boys even have the emblem of their favourite football club on their skull caps.

Look at pages 45 (bottom image) 46 and 47.

4. Describe the different skull caps you can see.

5. Jewish men are proud to wear their skull caps. Why?

6. Do you think it is acceptable to have the emblem of your favourite football team on your skull cap? Give reasons for your answer.
   *Total time allowed 20 minutes.*

**Briefing and Activity Sheet**

# Why are tefillin so important in Jewish worship?

**Photo Book reference**: Pages 45–46

### Tefillin (Phylactery)

- Jewish males wear tefillin for weekday prayers.
- Once a boy has had his Bar Mitzvah at 13 he will be expected to wear tefillin.
- Tefillin consist of two black leather boxes (one worn on the upper arm, the other on the head).
- Inside each box there are small scrolls.
- Written on the scrolls are passages from the Jewish Bible.
- These scrolls are specially written by hand by a trained scribe.
- The tefillin on the arm has all four passages written on one scroll.
- The tefillin on the head has four separate compartments.
- Each of the compartments contains a scroll with one of the passages written on it.
- The boxes are sewn up with sinews, i.e. tissue which unites muscle to bone.
- Everything must be made from the skins of kosher animals.
- The arm tefillin is fastened to the top of the arm (on the muscle) so that when the arm is straight it points to the heart, reminding the wearer that he must serve God with his heart.
- The head tefillin is fastened to the mid point of the forehead thus reminding the wearer that he must serve God with his mind.

Kosher means those foods which Jews are allowed to eat. They can only eat meat from animals which have cloven hooves and chew the cud, i.e. cattle and sheep, and from fish that have fins and scales. Also any meat must have been killed in a certain way which ensures that no pain was inflicted on the animal at all. So the skin from those kosher animals is the only skin which can be used for tefillin.

> 'And you shall bind them as a sign upon your hand and they shall be frontlets between your eyes.'
> *(Deuteronomy 6:8)*

*The tefillin are very special objects for a Jew. The scrolls are checked every three years and if any of the writing is faded it is rewritten – by a scribe.*

### Examine the evidence

Look at pages 45 and 46 which show Jewish boys wearing the tefillin.

1. Why is it important to worship God with your heart and mind? What does this mean exactly?

2. 'The wearing of the tefillin binds us together.' What do you think this means for the boys in the images?

3. Why do you think the writing on the scrolls is checked at regular intervals? What does this tell you about what is written?

4. Describe how the boys in the pictures look, for example proud, happy?
   *Total time allowed 30 minutes.*

## Briefing and Activity Sheet

# What is a mezuzah and why is it important to Jews?

**Photo Book reference**: Page 48

Deuteronomy 6:9 goes on to say:

*'And you shall write them upon the posts of your house and on your gates.'*

The word mezuzah means 'door-post' and Jews fix a mezuzah case containing a scroll, with the first two paragraphs of the Shema in it, to the door frame of their homes and synagogues.

> *Deuteronomy 6:4–5*
> 'Hear O Israel:
> The Lord our God, the Lord is One,
> And you shall love the Lord your God
> With all your heart, with all your soul,
> And with all your might.'

The two passages on the mezuzah scroll are Deuteronomy 6:4–9 and 11:13–21.
- A mezuzah scroll must be written, by hand, by a trained scribe on parchment.
- The parchment must come from the skin of a kosher animal.
- Many Jews have a mezuzah on the doorpost of every room in their house – apart from the toilet/bathroom.
- Indoors, some Jews do not place the mezuzah scroll into a mezuzah case. They simply wrap the scroll in plastic.
- The mezuzah is fixed to the doorpost on the right-hand side.
- Every three years the scroll is checked to make sure it is in good condition.
- The checking is done by a scribe or sometimes by a rabbi.

### Examine the evidence
The top image on page 48 shows a Jewish man kissing his fingers after touching the mezuzah. The bottom image is a close-up of the mezuzah case.

1. Why do you think the fingers are kissed after touching the mezuzah?

2. On the mezuzah case the first letter of the word 'Shaddai' meaning 'Almighty' is written. Look at it – on the top part of the mezuzah. Think about that word – why do you think Jews use it to describe their God? What idea does it give you about God?
*Total time allowed 10 minutes.*

3. Why do you think Jews have the text above from Deuteronomy 6:4–9 on the scroll? What does the text mean and why is it so important?
*Time allowed 10 minutes.*

Read what Aaron says about the mezuzah:

> 'When I go into my house or when I leave it I touch the mezuzah and then I kiss the fingers which have touched the mezuzah. It somehow comforts me to know that all Jews do this wherever they live and whoever they are. It reminds me that God is there, always present, always watching out for me. It also reminds me that Jews throughout history have fastened this to their doorposts and Jews in the future will do the same.'